Me Too!®

BEDTIME BIBLE STORIES

By
Tim Dowley

Illustrated by
Stephanie McFetridge Britt

CANDLE BOOKS

Contents

Noah

and the Ark Full of Animals

As everybody knows, the very first man and woman were named Adam and Eve. They lived together in a beautiful garden. But they had to leave the garden because they did wrong.

Adam and Eve had children.
And they sometimes did wrong things too.
And their children had children.
And they sometimes did wrong things.

"So many people are doing bad things," said God sadly. "So few are doing good. Perhaps I should destroy the world and all these bad things along with it."

But one good man was left on earth.
His name was Noah.
"Listen, Noah!" said God.
"I am going to send a great flood on the earth. It will destroy everything.
But I will save you and your family.
Build a great ship, called an ark,
so that you will all be safe."

So Noah did as God told him.
He cut down trees.
He sawed up wood.
He started to build a great ark.
Noah's sons were Ham, Shem, and Japheth.
They all helped him.
They cut, they sawed, and they hammered.

Noah's friends made fun of him.
"Why are you building a boat on dry land?"
they laughed. "You're crazy!"
But Noah went on building,
until at last his ark was finished.
It was the biggest, strongest boat ever
made.

Why did Noah build his ark so big?

Because God said, "Noah, you must take two of every creature on earth into the ark with you."

Now rain clouds were gathering.
So the animals and birds started to arrive two by two.
Noah made sure they all climbed inside the ark. And then God shut the door.

Soon the rain began to fall.
It rained as it had never rained before.
Lightning flashed.
Thunder roared.

And still it rained.
The water rose.
Before long, the ark was floating on the water.

And *still* it rained,
until water covered the whole earth.

But the ark floated safely on the water. And Noah, his family, and all the animals were safe and dry inside.

The rain kept on falling—
for forty days and forty nights.
Then, at last, it stopped.
Everyone inside the ark was glad.
Even the birds sang for joy.
But water still covered the land.

Noah opened the window in the ark.
He sent off a dove to try to find
somewhere to perch.
But the dove flew back.
There was only water
—*nowhere* to rest.

After a few days, Noah sent off the dove again.
"Perhaps she will find some dry land now," he said.
This time the dove came back with a green leaf in her beak.
She had found a tree above water.
Everyone was so happy!

At last the waters started to dry up.
The ark stopped floating and came
to rest high on a mountain.
Noah, his family, and all the creatures
left the giant ark.
And God said,
"I promise I will never again
flood the whole earth."

And God put a beautiful rainbow in the sky to remind us of his promise.

Question

What was the name of the good man who built the ark?

Prayer

God, thank you for rainbows and your promise never again to flood the whole earth.

Joseph
and the Pharaoh of Egypt

Joseph lived in the desert with his father and his brothers.
But Joseph's brothers grew very jealous of him.
One day they sold Joseph to some men who were passing by on camels.

These cruel men took Joseph on a long, long journey across the desert.
At last they arrived in the land of Egypt.
The men took Joseph to the market.

The men wanted to sell Joseph as a slave.
A man named Potiphar came to market.
When he saw Joseph,
he decided to buy him.
He wanted him as his slave.

Joseph worked very hard as Potiphar's slave.
He did what he was told,
and Potiphar trusted him.
But Mrs Potiphar told lies about Joseph.
She said he had done wrong.
Poor Joseph was thrown into prison
although he had done *nothing* wrong.

Even in prison Joseph behaved well.
Soon the jailer asked Joseph
to be his special helper.
Now Pharaoh was king of Egypt.
One day, two of his servants
were thrown into the prison.

One night, the two servants
both had strange dreams.
Joseph was clever at explaining dreams.
He told one servant his dream meant
Pharaoh was going to free him from
prison.
But he told the other servant his dream
meant Pharaoh was going to kill him.

And that's just what happened.
The first servant was freed,
and the other servant was killed.
The first servant had promised
to ask Pharaoh to free Joseph too.
But once he was free,
he forgot all about Joseph!

Then one night Pharaoh himself
had a strange dream.
In his dream he saw seven fat cows.
Suddenly seven skinny cows came out
of the river and gobbled up the fat cows.

The next night Pharaoh had
another strange dream.
In this dream he saw seven
good ears of corn.
Suddenly seven bad ears of corn
came and gobbled up
the good ears of corn!

Pharaoh was scared by his dreams.
He didn't know what they meant.
And Pharaoh's friends didn't know
what his dreams meant either.
Then, at last, Pharaoh's servant
remembered Joseph.

Pharaoh's servant ran to the prison.
He told Joseph to wash and
put on fresh, clean clothes.
He was going to meet Pharaoh,
the king of Egypt!

Pharaoh told Joseph his dreams.
"Both dreams mean exactly the same thing," said Joseph. "There will be seven years with good harvests and plenty of food. Then seven years of bad harvests when everyone will go hungry."
Pharaoh looked very worried.

"But listen," said Joseph,
"You must make sure your people
store food from the good harvests.
Then when the bad harvests come,
there will still be enough to eat."
"That's a great idea!" said Pharaoh,
who already looked more cheery.
"And you must find a clever man
to see that this is done," said Joseph.

"I know just the man!" said Pharaoh. "Joseph—you are that wise and clever man. The job is yours."

Question

Why did Pharaoh say that Joseph was a wise and clever man?

Prayer

Thank you, God, that you are with me when I'm in trouble.

The Boy in the Basket

Joseph's family lived in Egypt for many years.
His children had children.
His children's children had children.

They were called the Israelites.
Then another Pharaoh came along.
He did not like them.

"These Israelites are an awful nuisance,"
Pharaoh said one day.
"What shall we do about them?"
asked his top men.
"Make them our slaves!
They will build buildings for us."

So the Israelites had to work
for Pharaoh as slaves.
But Pharaoh said,
"There are just *too* many of them!"
"What shall we do?" asked his soldiers.
"Throw all their baby boys into the river!"
So they did.

But one mother saved her baby boy. When the soldiers came, she hid him away.

Her son Aaron and her daughter Miriam helped her.
But before long the baby grew too big to hide.

"I have a clever plan," the mother told Aaron and Miriam.

"We'll make a basket from reeds," she said.
"We'll make it so that it will float.
It will be like a tiny boat."
And they did.

One morning, Miriam and her mother carried the baby to the river.
They gently laid the baby in the basket and hid it among the bulrushes.

Then Miriam hid too.
She wanted to see what would happen
to her baby brother.

Miriam waited and waited.
Then she heard voices.
She peeked out.

She could hardly believe her eyes!
It was the princess of Egypt,
coming to bathe in the river.

Then the princess noticed the little basket among the bulrushes.
"What is that?" she asked her maid.
"Bring it here!"
The maid brought the basket.
The princess looked in the basket and saw the baby boy.

"It must be one of the babies that were supposed to be thrown into the river," said the princess. "Isn't he just *beautiful!*"

Miriam sprang from her hiding place. "Your majesty," she began shyly. "Would you like a nurse for the baby?"

"Why, yes—what a good idea!"

Without another word, Miriam ran home.
"Mother—the princess wants you
to nurse the baby!"
At first her mother didn't understand.
Miriam told her all that had happened.
Then her mother hurried with her
to meet the princess.

"I've found a nurse for the baby," said Miriam.
"Will you look after this beautiful baby for me?" the princess asked the mother.

"I shall make him my son," said the princess.
"When he is old enough, bring him to the palace to live as a prince."

So Miriam and her mother
took the baby safely home again.
They would take care of him for the
princess.

One day, when he was no longer a baby, Miriam and her mother took the little boy to the palace.

The princess hugged him joyfully.

"I will call you Moses," she said.

So Moses was brought up as a prince in Pharaoh's palace. But he never forgot his own people, the Israelites.

Question

Where did the princess find the baby?

Prayer

Thank you, God, that you looked after Moses. Look after me, too.

The Boy Who Listened to God

When he grew up, Moses led his people,
the Israelites, to a land of their own.
There, in a place called Shiloh,
stood God's special tent.
Every year the people came there
for a great festival.

One man came with his wife, Hannah.
She was very sad
because she had no children.
How she longed for a little boy!

One day Hannah went into God's Tent.
"Dear Lord," she prayed, "give us a baby boy. We promise to give him back to serve you."
Eli the priest was watching.
"May God give you what you ask," he said.

God *did* give Hannah what she asked for.
She had a baby boy named Samuel.
When he was old enough,
she took him to Eli.
"Here is the son I prayed for," she said.
"I have brought him to serve God,
as I promised."

So Samuel came to work with Eli
in God's Tent.
He helped the priests.
He filled the oil lamps.
And he learned to read.

Each year at festival time,
Hannah visited Samuel.
She brought him a new coat.
Samuel grew up happy and strong.

One night Samuel heard a
voice as he was sleeping.
Samuel thought it was Eli.
He ran to him.
"Here I am; you called."

"No, I didn't," said Eli,
"Go back to bed."
The same thing happened
three times.

Then Eli knew it must be God calling
Samuel's name.
He told Samuel, "Next time, say,
'Speak Lord—I am listening.' "
That night Samuel heard the call again.
"Speak Lord," he said. "I am listening."
God told him that Eli's sons
had done wrong things.
They would be punished.
Samuel and Eli were very sad.

Things turned out just as God said.
Enemies fought the Israelites.
They burned down God's Tent and carried off the golden ark.
And Eli's two sons were killed.

When he grew up, Samuel ruled his people.
He sorted out their arguments.
He explained God's ways to them.
One day the people said,
"We want a real king to rule us."
So Samuel set out to find
a king for his people.

There was one young man
who was taller than anyone else.
His name was Saul.
One day his father said,
"I've lost my donkeys.
Will you go and find them?"
So Saul set out to search
for his father's donkeys.

Saul searched everywhere,
but his father's donkeys were
nowhere to be found.
"Samuel lives near here," said his servant.
"He's very wise. Let's ask him."
As soon as he saw Saul,
Samuel thought he should be king.
So he invited Saul to a great feast.

At the feast, Saul found, to his surprise, that he was sitting in the best seat. "The people of Israel need you as king," said Samuel. "And don't worry about the donkeys—they've all been found!"

So Saul returned home and
worked at his father's home.
He waited for Samuel to call for him.
Then he would be made king.

At last the day arrived.

"Behold your king," said Samuel.

How the people cheered!

Question

What was Saul looking for when Samuel met him?

Prayer

Lord, help me to listen to you, like Samuel.

The Shepherd Boy and His Sling

When Saul first became king of Israel,
he was a good king.
But later he did wrong things.
Samuel grew sorry
that he had made Saul king.

God sent Samuel to find another king.
"Go to Bethlehem," he said.
"You'll find a man named Jesse.
One of his sons will be king."

When Samuel arrived, he said to Jesse,
"I'm giving a great feast.
Invite all your sons!"

Jesse's sons came to their father's house. Samuel looked them all over carefully.

But none of them seemed *quite* right.
"Are all your sons here?"
he asked Jesse, a bit puzzled.

"All except David," said Jesse.
"But he's much too young
to come to your feast."
"Where is he?" asked Samuel.

"He's in the field taking care of the sheep."

"Then send for him too," said Samuel.

As soon as he saw David, Samuel knew God wanted him to be king.
So he gave David a special blessing.
But it wasn't time yet for David to be made king.

So David went back to the fields
to protect his sheep.
Sometimes he played his harp.
Once he killed a lion.
Once he killed a bear.

Saul was still king of Israel.
Sometimes he was very, very miserable.
"Would you like the shepherd boy David to play for you?" a servant asked.
"He plays the harp so beautifully."
So David played his harp,
and Saul felt much happier.

The enemies of Israel came to fight.
One of their soldiers was the biggest
giant you could ever imagine.
His name was Goliath.
Every day he shouted,
"Isn't there *anyone* in Israel
brave enough to fight me?"

The Israelites were terrified.
No one dared fight Goliath.
When David heard Goliath shouting,
he asked, "Who is going to fight this giant?"
No one answered.

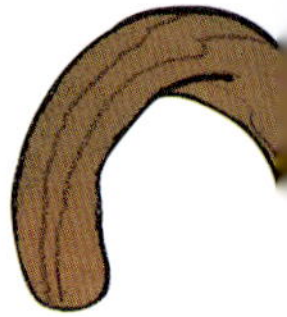

So David said to King Saul,
"I'll go and fight this giant."
Saul gave him a sword and a helmet.
But they were much too heavy.
So David picked five smooth stones
from a stream.
Then he went to face Goliath.

The giant roared with laughter.
"I'm not a dog you can chase off!"
he shouted.

But David just put a stone in his sling,
whirled it around and flung it at the giant.
The stone hit Goliath on his forehead.
He crashed to the ground.
The Israelites cheered and cheered!

King Saul was very pleased with David.
"You will be one of my captains,"
he said.
And David became great friends
with Saul's son, Jonathan.

But one day Saul heard people say,
"David has killed a lot more enemies than Saul!"
Saul was furious!
He flung a spear at David
—and it barely missed him.
David had to run away.

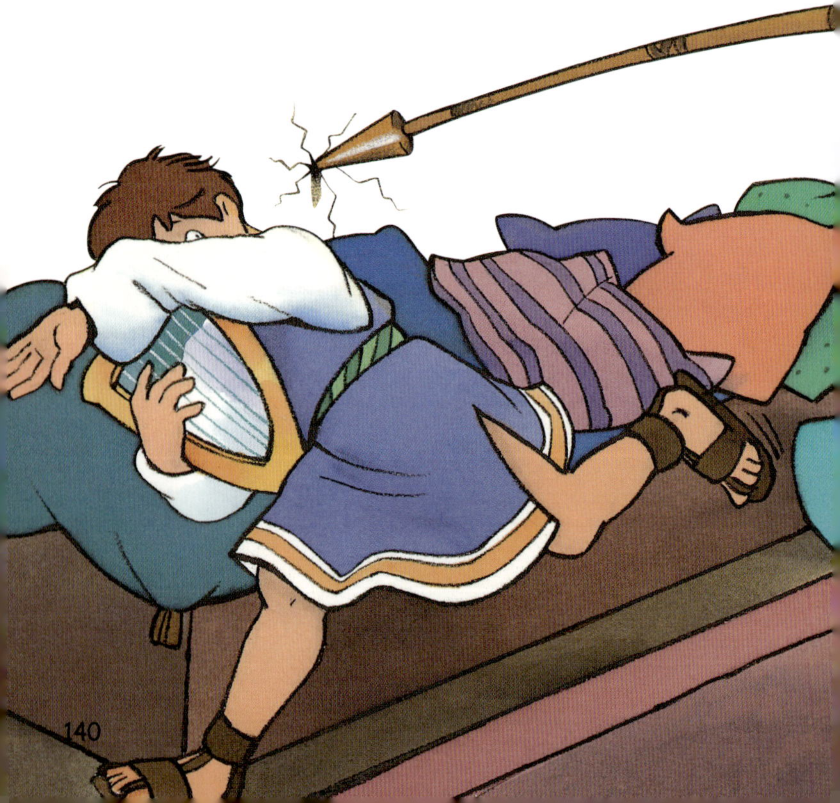

Soon after, Saul died in a terrible battle.
David was made king.
The shepherd boy became king of Israel.

Question
What was the name of David's friend?

Prayer
Lord, help me to be brave like David.

Lost and Found

You remember the story of Christmas?
Baby Jesus was born
in a stable in Bethlehem.
When Jesus was born,
wicked King Herod told his soldiers,
"Go and kill all boy babies."

Mary and Joseph heard this,
and ran away from Bethlehem.

Mary and Joseph took baby Jesus
far away to the land of Egypt.
They stayed there until they heard
it was safe to return home.
Then they set out on the long journey
to Nazareth, where they lived.

At last they saw some little houses
in the distance.
There was Nazareth, among the hills!

Jesus grew up with Mary and Joseph
in their little house in Nazareth.
Joseph was a carpenter.
Jesus helped him in his workshop,
sawing and hammering.

Sometimes Jesus played with other children.
Sometimes he watched the shepherd leading his sheep.

And sometimes he watched women get water from the well.

When he was old enough,
Jesus went to school.
Teachers told him about God's law.
He listened carefully and remembered well.
How proud his mother was!

One day, when Jesus was helping Mary, she said,

"We are going to a great festival in Jerusalem. You are old enough to come with us."

So they set off on the long road to Jerusalem.
There were lots of other people on the journey.
They were all looking forward to seeing the great city of Jerusalem.

At last they arrived at the wonderful city.
Joseph and Mary took Jesus
to the beautiful, golden temple.
He met men who explained God's Law.

All too soon, the festival was over.
Mary and Joseph left for home.
Mary didn't see Jesus all day.
She thought he was playing
with the other children.
But night came, and he was
nowhere to be found!

So Mary and Joseph went back to Jerusalem to try to find Jesus. They asked everyone they met, "Have you seen our son Jesus?" But no one knew where he was.

"Perhaps we should look in the temple," said Mary.
So they made their way back to the temple .
And there, at last, they saw Jesus.
He was with the wise old teachers of the Law, asking them questions.

"Why didn't you go back with us?" asked Mary. "We've been so worried!"
"I had to be here, in my Father's house," Jesus said. "I'm learning God's ways."

Then Jesus returned with Joseph and Mary to the little town of Nazareth. But he kept thinking about the things he had heard in the temple.

Question

Where did Mary and Joseph find Jesus?

Prayer

Lord Jesus, help me to understand your teachings.

Jesus Helps a Sad Father

This little girl lived in a fishing village, beside the Lake of Galilee.
She was waiting for her father, Jairus, to come home.

At last she saw her father
coming up the hill.
She ran to meet him.
They went home for dinner.

But when the little girl woke up
in the morning, she didn't feel well.
Her head ached and she felt hot.
Her mother tucked her into bed again.

The doctor came,
but the little girl didn't get better.
Two or three days went by,
and she was worse still.
Jairus was *terribly* worried.
"I've heard Jesus is here,"
said his wife.
"He's been healing many people."

Jairus rushed out of the house.
A man said, "Jesus is across the lake
—we're waiting for him here."

Jairus looked anxiously across the water.

As soon as Jesus' boat landed,
Jairus pushed through the crowd.
"You must come to heal my little girl,"
he said. "I think she's dying."
"Let's go," said Jesus.

The crowds followed Jesus to Jairus's house.
One woman in the crowd had been sick for twelve years.
The doctors couldn't help her.
She longed for Jesus to heal her.

This woman was very timid.
She didn't dare ask Jesus to help.
She just touched his robe.
Jesus stopped.
"Who touched me?" he asked.

Everyone stopped.
After a moment,
the woman came forward.
"I knew if I touched you,"
she said, "I would get better."
Jesus said,
"You trusted me
—so you were healed."

Just then, a man came from Jairus's
house.
"Don't bother Jesus now," the man said.
"Your little girl is dead."
But Jesus kept walking.
"Just believe in me," he told Jairus.

When they arrived at Jairus's house,
they heard people crying.
"Don't cry," said Jesus.
"The little girl isn't dead—she's sleeping."
But they laughed at him.

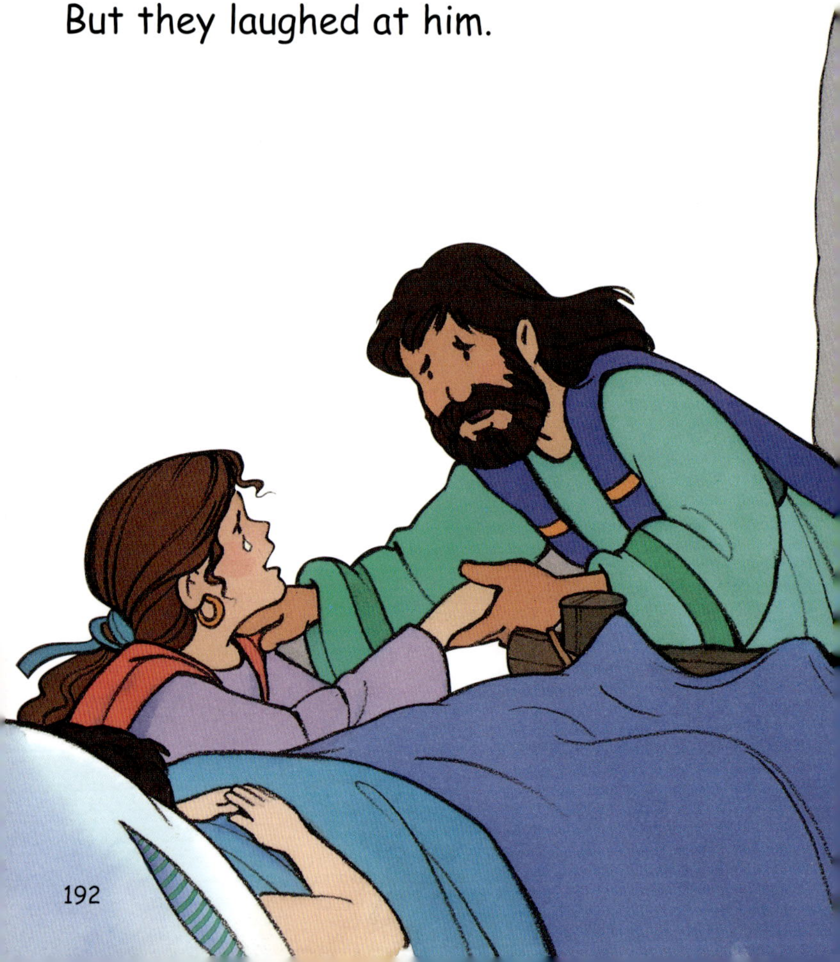

Jesus went into the house.
Gently, he took the little girl's hand.
"Child, get up now!" he said.

The little girl opened her eyes.
Her mother and father were so happy.
"Get the little girl something to eat," said Jesus.
Once she'd had some food and a drink, she felt much better.
Jairus thanked Jesus.

Jesus left the happy family together. They never forgot that wonderful day.

Question

What did Jesus tell the girl's parents to give her?

Prayer

Thank you that Jesus is able to take care of me.

The Stranger Who Helped

This is a story that Jesus told.
There was once a man who was on a journey from Jerusalem to Jericho.

The road was very lonely.

Suddenly thieves jumped on him.
They beat him up
and stole everything he had—
even his clothes.
Then they ran off.

The man lay hurt in the road.
He groaned with pain.
At last he heard footsteps.
It was a priest.

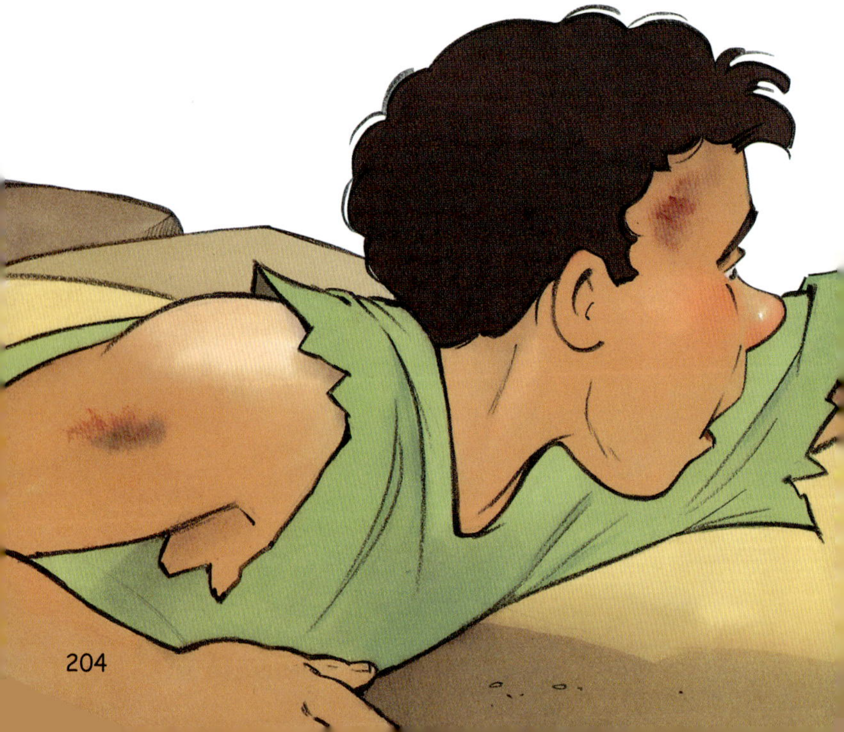

"Help!" he called, weakly. "Help me, please!" But the priest crossed to the other side of the road and went on his way.

Then another man came along.
He worked in the temple in Jerusalem.

He looked at the man lying in the road.
Then he stood up and walked off.

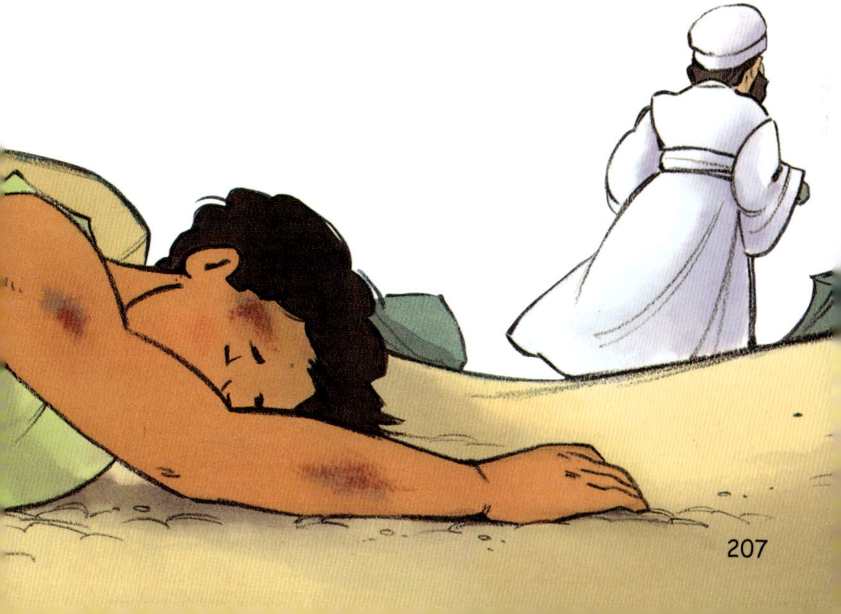

The wounded man heard more steps.
This time it was a foreigner!
The man came over to him.
"Let me help," he said.
"I have medicine and bandages with me."

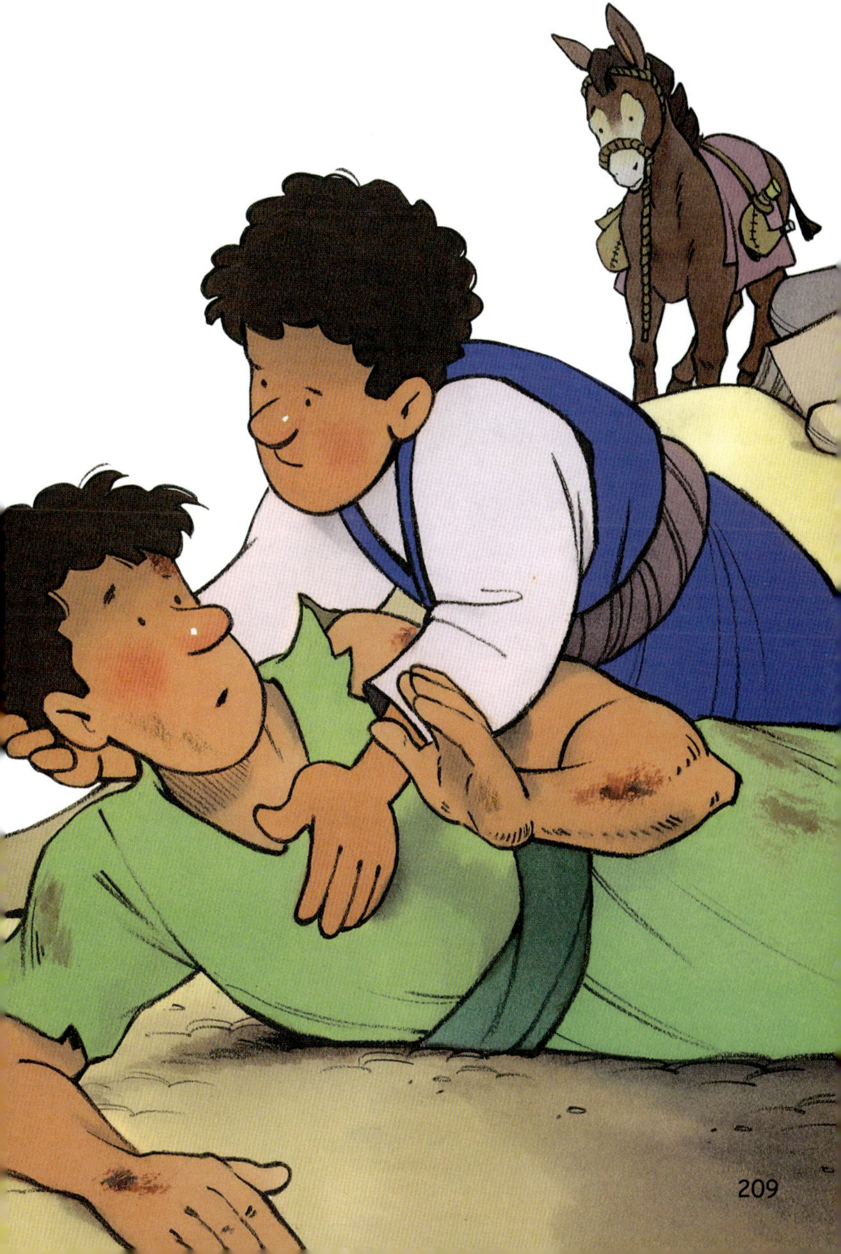

The stranger cleaned his wounds
as best he could.
Then he carefully lifted the poor man
onto his donkey.
"I'll get you to a hotel
where you can rest until you're well,"
said the stranger.

The stranger made sure
the man was comfortable in the hotel.
He even paid for his room!

After he told this story, Jesus asked, "Which of the three —the priest, the man from the temple or the stranger—pleased God most?"

Question

Which of the three people pleased God the most?

Prayer

Lord, help me to love and help other people.

The Son Who Came Back

There once was a man with two sons.
One day the younger son said to his father, "Give me my share of your money."
Then he left home and went far away.
He wasted all his money on parties.

It wasn't long before he'd used up all his money, and all his new friends disappeared. He got so hungry that he took the first job he could find.

He looked after a herd of pigs.
He even started to eat the pigs' food!
He was *so* miserable.

One day he came to his senses.
He said to himself,
"My father's *servants* live better than this!
I'll go home and tell dad
that I'll work as his servant."
So he left the pigs
and started the long walk home.

His father had never stopped
thinking of him.
When he saw his boy coming,
he ran and hugged him.
"Give him my best clothes
and a fine gold ring," he said.
"My son was lost—now he's found."

The father gave a great feast for his boy.
But his older son was very angry.
"I never left home," he said.
"And I've always done as I'm told.
But you never gave me a feast!"

“You’ve always been here to share my things,” his father said. “But your brother was lost—and now he’s found. We *must* be happy!”

Question

What job did the younger son do while he was away?

Prayer

Lord, thank you for Bible stories that help me learn more about you.

The Boy Who Shared His Lunch

A little boy lived near Lake Galilee.
He lived with his family in a square, white house.
He often caught fish in Lake Galilee.

One day he brought home two little fish that he had caught.

"Mother, can we cook them?" he asked.

"Yes, we'll cook them," she said.

"You can have them for lunch tomorrow."

The next morning the boy and his little sister were up early.
As they played on the hillside, they saw many people walking by.
"Where are you going?" asked the boy.

"Haven't you heard?" asked a woman.
"Jesus is coming across the lake."
"Who's Jesus?" asked the boy.
"Oh—he's great!" she said.
"He tells wonderful stories
and he does wonderful things."
"Can we come and see him?"
"Of course! Just ask your mother."

The boy ran home with his sister.
"Can I go and see Jesus he asked?"
"Of course you can," his mother replied.
"But your sister's a bit too young."
"Can I take my fish for lunch?"
"Yes! And I'll put in five little loaves of bread as well!"

So the little boy joined the people walking over the hills to meet Jesus.

"Is Jesus still here?" he asked a man. "I don't want to miss him."

"Yes—there he is," said the man, and pointed up the hill.

Then the little boy saw Jesus.
He was talking to some people.
There was a man with a hurt leg
who needed healing.
What a kind face Jesus had!

Lots of sick people came to Jesus
and he healed them.
Then all the people sat down
and Jesus began to tell them
wonderful stories.
The boy listened carefully.

Everyone was so busy listening to Jesus they didn't notice it was getting late. The sun was setting.

Suddenly everyone felt hungry.
One of Jesus' friends said,
"How can we feed everyone?
There are no shops to buy food."

"Has anybody here brought food?" shouted another of Jesus' friends. Everyone shook their heads. Then up jumped the boy. He took his lunch basket to Jesus' friend.

The man took him to Jesus.
"Here's a boy with five loaves
and two fishes," he told Jesus.
Jesus gave thanks for the food.
Then he broke up the bread and fishes.
Jesus' friends gave it to the people.

The funny thing was,
there was enough for everyone!
Somehow, Jesus turned one boy's lunch
into supper for everyone.
The little boy was very pleased
he had given Jesus his loaves and fishes.

At last everyone had eaten enough.
The people began to go home,
tired but very happy.
Jesus' friends started to clean up.
They collected twelve whole baskets
of leftovers.

It was dark when the boy reached home. His mother was worried.
"I'll never forget what happened today," he told her. "It was the best day of my life!"

Question
What did the boy give Jesus?

Prayer
Thank you, Jesus, that you can use me as your helper.

All these stories come from the Bible.

You can read them for yourself.

Noah and the Ark Full of Animals: Genesis 6:9–8:22

Joseph and the Pharaoh of Egypt: Genesis 37, 39–45

The Boy in the Basket: Exodus 2:1–10

The Boy Who Listened to God: 1 Samuel 3–4, 8–10

The Shepherd Boy and His Sling: 1 Samuel 16–18

Lost and Found: Matthew 2:13–23; Luke 2:41–52

Jesus Helps a Sad Father: Luke 8:40–56

The Stranger Who Helped: Luke 10:25–37

The Son Who Came Back: Luke 15:11–32

The Boy Who Shared His Lunch: John 6:1–13

Text by Tim Dowley
Illustrations by Stephanie McFetridge Britt

This edition published in 2011 by Candle Books,
a publishing imprint of Lion Hudson plc

Distributed in the UK by Marston Book Services Ltd,
PO Box 269, Abingdon, Oxon, OX14 4YN
ISBN 978 1 85985 895 0 (UK)

Distributed in the USA by Kregel Publications,
PO Box 2607, Grand Rapids, Michigan, 49501
ISBN 978 1 85985 918 6 (US)

Worldwide co-edition produced by Lion Hudson plc,
Wilkinson House, Jordan Hill Road, Oxford, OX2 8DR
Tel: +44 (0)1865 302750
Fax: +44 (0)1865 302757
Email: coed@lionhudson.com
www.lionhudson.com

First printing January 2011 (manufacturer LH06), China